resume drowning

resume drowning © 2002 Jon Paul Fiorentino

Acknowledgements: *dark leisure, The Queen Street Quarterly, You & Your Bright Ideas: New Montreal Writing* (Montreal: Véhicule Press, 2001), *Poetic Stream Three* (Maxville ON: above/ground press, 2000)

cauldron books 3
series editor: rob mclennan

Cover art: from the "I Want" series, gel transfer on MDF,
        copyright © 2001 Rosemary Bockner
Author photo by Tara Flanagan
Design and in-house editing by the publisher, Joe Blades
Printed and bound in Canada by Sentinel Printing, Yarmouth NS
Simultaneously published as BJP eBook 41, ISBN 1-896647-95-2 (PDF)

No part of this publication may be reproduced, stored in a retrieval system or transmitted, in any form or by any means, without the prior written permission of the publisher or, in the case of photocopying or other reprographic copying, a licence from the Canadian Copyright Licencing Agency, 1900-One Yonge St, Toronto ON M5E 1E5. Tel 416 868-1620, 1-800-893-5777, fax 416 868-1621, admin@cancopy.com www.cancopy.com

The publisher acknowledges the support of the Canada Council for the Arts and the New Brunswick Culture and Sport Secretariat-Arts Development Branch.

cauldron books
A series edited by Ottawa writer/editor/publisher rob mclennan. Named after the Celtic idea of the cauldron as the keeper & dispenser of wisdom & knowledge. The series will focus not only on worthwhile collections of poetry, but on single author collections of essays, as writing on writing. cauldron books are published by Broken Jaw Press. rob may be reached at <az421@freenet.carleton.ca>

Broken Jaw Press
Box 596 Stn A
Fredericton NB E3B 5A6
Canada

www.brokenjaw.com
jblades@nbnet.nb.ca
tel / fax 506 454-5127

National Library of Canada Cataloguing in Publication Data
Fiorentino, Jon Paul
      Resume drowning / Jon Paul Fiorentino.

(Cauldron books ; 3)
Poems.
Also issued in electronic format.
ISBN 1-896647-94-4

      I. Title. II. Series.

PS8561.I585R48 2002   C811'.54   C2002-903389-6
PR9199.3.F5325R48 2002

resume drowning

Jon Paul Fiorentino

cauldron books 3

Fredericton • Canada

For Tara

contents

section 1: resume drowning
introductory sapphics 9
lyric 1 10
lyric 2 29
lyric 3 36
lyric 3.1 46
lyric 3.2 47
lyric 3.3 48
lyric 3.4 49
lyric 3.5 50
lyric 3.6 51
lyric 3.7 52
lyric 3.8 53
lyric 3.9 54
lyric 4 55
lyric 4.1 56
lyric 4.2 57
lyric 4.3 58
sonnet 1 59
sonnet 1.01 60

section 2: semisorry
semisorry 63
heliotrope 67
lament 70
ode to my valium 73
pharmacy 74
history 75
metaflow 76
remember the last time 77
slip 78
vendor 85
immaculate worming 87
blooming 88
floral 89
soundtracking 91

"it was lovely just waiting" 92
freon 93
winter is listening 94

postscript 95

section 1
resume drowning

*Nobody heard him, the dead man,
But still he lay moaning:
I was much further out than you thought
And not waving but drowning.*
　　　　—Stevie Smith

I don't know what to do. I'm in two minds.
　　　　—Sappho　　(trans. Robert Chandler)

introductory sapphics

tainted sapphics come to me
through my filthy latticed window
the stars mutter in fractured verse
        come down to the street

steven, you never come down you
never cease the funereal moaning
come round my stereo, take my pills
        uptake the dream

mother, never mind my lips, my
creaking lips, the traipsing speech
that scars, instead turn your eyes to
        weeping tasteless verse

muses huffing in the alleyway
or they split their dime bags open
or wake the lowly poet-drones who
        pine away their breath

mother, i cannot lift my hand
i cannot write a word

steven, i am senseless
i cannot breathe

lyric 1

the grip of winnipeg
      sad sleet concrete

the grip of familial shame

whispering through the
structure of chain link
come here—
let me tell you something sick

whenever you want me
i'm already taken

delicate and jaundiced
self-loathing and rapidly aging

the grip of suburban familiarity
the grip of already being classed

whenever you want me
i'll be on regent avenue retailing

if you offer me one night
i will apologize and explain that
i'm already shameful

don't sleep just yet

you don't tell me
who you are
but you stand there
on my driveway
problematically suburban

don't tell anyone about this
discourse

it can be done in the expansive living room
it can be done behind the challenged buildings of the exchange district
it can be done behind the trash bins
it can be done in front of an ATM
it can be done in and out of style
it can be done in and out of rhythm with off-rhymes—lyric and sad

fixing, retailing, tripping

and meta-tripping

it can be done in silence

the poem bp posits
escapes me

aural perspiration
punctuating the room
trying to emote
a modular filmic tract
and bp growls

madness is language is how you use it
there are many ways of both ways

winnipeg pines, spineless
drowning in its
idiosyncratic history

remember when you spent that year in bed?
remember how freeing it was to escape to valium
and to not open your eyes for days?

yeah that was great
can we go again?
can we?
can we?

remember the girl you thought
you couldn't live without?
and then, in bed, you realized,
sedated and looking fabulous,
that you didn't care as much as the day before

                        i'm taking a day off
                        i'm taking a day just for myself
                        to stop myself
                        to self-myself

on regent avenue you can catch
a fleeting glimpse of me
retailing to the point of
servicide

it's entirely my fault all the time
the customer is always trite

i thought
i was alone
i was sure
that
no one
was around
please don't say a word

it has been seven years with the same old high
seven straight years of observational drivel

from the back lanes
of an unwashed transcona
to the living room couch—
a historical landscape

fixated on place
underplaced

i'd love to take you home
but i haven't got one
i have no place to drown

[could you possibly
drown me?]

sinking like a stoned one
in the mattress
under extrapolations
of the lyric i

emily wakes beside me
her sour breath
penetrating my dream
emily wakes
and whispers:

Drowning is not so pitiful
As the attempt to rise

i hear her and i rise

which valium stream did i take?
which sleep did i sleep?
you don't know

emily is silent
bp is grinning

the lyric you comes all over home
the lyric you sings waste, trills melancholic
the lyric you fails to dance across the nape of my neck
fails to deliver me into the ethereal

lyric we are not home right now please leave

the lyric i is singing hyperkinetic
the lyric i is killing his cosmology
the lyric i is sleeping

trying to distinguish the subtle difference between cursing and versing
trying to rewrite the difference

your lucid smile
the amber streetlights
the damp air
like a menthol cigarette
tickling the throat
your breath like ether
your speech fragmented
and real

the difference between us—
expressed in adolescent telephone calls
that never end

impossible equations
linguistic choice
aesthetic order

thank god for you—
you wasted my time with me
a brilliant time waster

resume drowning when the whimper begins
resume drowning when the dreams turn manic
resume drowning when the phone rings
resume drowning when texts merge
resume drowning when in doubt

my head hit the pillow
and shattered like brittle glass
and then i rose
like historical tragedy
i rose

life begins when the vial is empty
and in an unremarkable office
somewhere in the city
a therapist can feel me coming

resume drowning when memory persists
resume drowning when waving

a lyric can kill you—
if it stays inside
like a parasitic dickinson

stay inside tonight like a literary insect
stay inside tonight like familial violence
stay inside tonight like every other night

shh

she called me
from wherever she was
to exorcize me

day in day out
she ripped the phantoms
from my exaggerated stomach
bloated and fabulous

    what's new?
new pills. coming home?
    i can't
i can't either

she called me simply to call me
to practice a sickly interpellation

    are you still...
as still as can be

i'm taking a moment for myself
i'm taking a moment and placing in on my tongue
and letting it unfold

i'm calling the ambulance just in case
i care about my health

but enough about me
how are we doing?

invoking linguistic resistance
singing home as if it existed

home is a system and it never works
if you're not home

i try to think what bp thot
emily suggests a certain hymn
i never listen

lay me down in a simple bedsit
let me sink into the soundless ethereal

or
sedate me in a sleeping bag
kill me with performance

stevie is waving
and plath has her head
in the oven again
in a grand poetic gesture
confessional and sessional
they hover around my bed
we roll our eyes simultaneously

this child was born melancholic
unpacked and eighteen years old
and now in the dry heat
the luminous summer
he stays in bed all day
writing lyrics
and the poets tend to him

emily unmotherly
tuck me in
implode me

this system of home is where
the jaundiced boy howls
pushed, thrushed

the world tastes like
bitter pills without coating

there is no fight or flight
only rest
pseudo-eternal

systemic winnipeg
holds me down
the wind just howls

i am what fails to drown—
bp's insistent possiblism
emily's sour breath
the mark of winnipeg
the remarked palimpsest
appropriated and sick
and adrienne introduces "we are"
into the bedsit landscape

it can be done in plurality
resume drowning when needed or every twelve hours
and i'll get back to you just as soon as we rise

lyric 2

you possess me

living between us

i'm coming down perpetually

      cover me with your dreams

you chill me

you keep me living

on the hardest days

your ghosts keep us going

      long may they live

you are beautiful when you sleep:

the escapist twitch of the eye your grin, a hook into the unconscious

this is why i stay awake   waxing academic   muttering hymns

to taste your kinetic sleep—bittersweet
to watch you wake uninspired and haunted

this is where i hail you into the illocutionary speech act
this is where i employ my only poetic trick to impress you [temporarily]
this is where i abort

your eyes still shut
the bed still and hypothetical
my skin jaundice and hypothermic

switching topics to the dreams we sin to each other

believe me when i tell you that i need you
when you sleeptalk to me
in audibility and in coherence

sing me to sleep
sleep me to dream
dream me to verse
verse me to serve

dreaming of
linguistic choice

wake up jonny
wake up jonny
good night jonny

i know it's time to spark another up
it's always time

the cats tumbling in the early morning haze
the pigeons recoiling at our window

we are
motionless
shattered
and content

and as problematic as it sounds
i don't mind if you possess me

you consistently remind me
that i am living

on the astral plane
on the academic plane
in the pastoral psychosis
in the esoteric stream

i am dreaming of possession
the kind that defines
and the kind that defies
and the kind that i project
in urban phantasy

possess me in silence
possess me in stasis
possess me in statistics
possess me in my lacanian sleepwalking my impenetrable self-
reflexivity   my sleep dis order

you with your chattering temporal tantrums
you with your subtle politicking
you with your heightened sense of responsibility
you with your need to feel me
you with your suicidal face—emotive and real

you with your catatonic whispers
you with your iambic drivel
you with your angelic fragments

possessing me until the world ends

the way the world ends: a phantastical eradication of binaries linguistic freedom and
coherence
the gods whimpering a canonical hymn   the sound is not persuasive
any more
you and i are perched like tourists

and the world ends
and you still possess me
and once again i am wrong about things
but i don't mind

you are the accidental gestures of sappho
the space that suggests disobedience

[   ] to see you
and [   ] under stars that whimper our cosmologies.

in assiniboine park
while claiming ownership of trees
and documenting an entire conversation
with a thick black marker
on the sidewalk
speaking in teenage angst
this is when the world ended for us
we whispered "no thanks" to time and space

and here we are
me, sick like the stars
and you, as always
possessing me

lyric 3

      home stretches above the convenience stores and endless suburban stills

and i am here
the spinster on a bender in a couch cradle and static clinging
to what i thought of as youth

we used to cruise the ghost city at night   rolling our eyes at the imaginary pedestrians and now as we sit singular with death crooning at our filthy window

it is impossible not to be nostalgic

        for the days of self-medication

      come into form and place me outside   where i can sit
quietly, observe

trilling the lyric i until the world heaves

come out into this outcome where you and i re-stitch memory and restrict it to us

outcoming and slumming

we slip into a nondescript street and declare ourselves urban and contemporary
      and therefore justified in our persistent self-gaze

where can we trill?

where can we indulge in muse poisoning?

screeching slippage all over the silent streets

swallowing prescriptive serum

catatonic and bashful

fulsome chiming

the bell tolls

verse telling trilling filling

unfair mystic

coated capsule

repugnant slippage

fulsome slippage

some slippery

stitch

i never got a chance to stray

    that is to say we never got a chance

    to stray from our bodies

mind you

we never finished anything

so come out in verse inversed and consumed and flattered and flattened

come out in verse so that i can

that is to say we can

if i never come   then the air just   wasn't worth
breathing

the fragile home is wilting

in the frigid, condensed night
the eyes close
the eyes roll

    here's the intangible beauty of making it accessible
here's the harsh lyric swallow, the thrush

the fragile home sits sighing

unsure of the very notion of geography

    here's the decorative spectrum
here's the absence of knowing exactly what to do
here's the pen and the paper and the pills and the fear
    breathing   staying
    in default mode

where would you take me
if you had the chance?
you are home and you are wilting

the town is stitched to the city
the world is unravelling

we are just fine

the obscenities are what bind us

the whiplash of cash

the bipolar familial links that define and bind and whine

the comical mating calls from corporations

the inbuilt wilt

miles and miles of similes
something like home

lyric 3.1

if i ever wanted to kill my gender
it would be now
but i don't now
i would however
like to
lull it to
sleep in seduction
wake it up in ether
and stretch it across
a suburban street
for everyone to tread on

lyric 3.2

behind your back   your shadow taunts you with reflections of your reflections

in your mirror staged half life   your shadow shatters

this is the split screen   that leads to the writing life
    the writing life irreverent letters laced and symphonic

the words wilt
          memory insists it is real

in the unbearable sensory weather we transmit stories that trip up the reader implode the author

in the murderous self-loathing of adulthood
your shadow is politicking   and the shrill home is ethereal   and undergraduate is the inversed syntax
calling home breaks up the family
the family breaks up
i'm calling

lyric 3.3

yet bound when i ask you
frigid and vitriolic is your text
      less than whole

consuming and consummating   under the abject
ceiling
coming down gently so ask me to traipse and stutter and verse
so ask me to

rest under dimly lit stars
yet boundless

under the tragic ceiling

lyric 3.4

around those bars and in those   back lanes conducive to violence
and apparitions
        we stranded ourselves amid   rusting cars and elusive
dreams of what it could possibly mean to sin
and politely breaking in   appropriating obscure objects from the
back seat or glove compartment

the streetlights wilt and mourn our absence   now
                                                    we are professional
    failures

breaking into words feebly   always leaving empty-handed
sadly conceptually stranded

and most of all afraid of being afraid

afraid of speaking in the present tense

and ultimately tense at the thought of going back there
in the light of early morning

where undriven cars sit patiently in their rust   waiting, pining
for us

we are always leaving there
always around

twinned we sinned

lyric 3.5

i have slipped into the classism of dreams tonight
dreaming into the crystalline leisure class
i am only honest in rhythm
i am cataclysmic and suicidal
my perceptual tangent is here tonight

the world of academia dreams to me
the unread libraries wail
the existence of knowing but not living

now son, there is verse
and there is *verse*
and the unread libraries
groan and sit impatiently

i am waiting for the wilting
the seduction of persistent dreams
and the fear of a dream coming true

lyric 3.6

i know that the best part of knowing is the novelty

slipping into the ontological
out of the particularity of the sensual moment

the scent of the unkempt summer lawn
that brings the unkempt child
to this and
what is this?

and what is this elusive reflection
dancing along the tinted window
of the car that never leaves
its suburban cradle?

lyric 3.7

and now all experience
seems to grow out of the jagged bliss
of little shadows playing with
a sense of desperation
hiding from anything parental

little shadows skeletal
drones meditating and
levitating silently in ownership
above expansive suburban lots

the false mythology of growth
has always possessed you
because you breathe its air
and you see yourself
in its unfinished basements
lethargic lawns and
patchwork concrete

lyric 3.8

the pressure of static is here my love [sic]
in the canonical verbiage of now
in the pixels that shatter
the cold years
the multinational years

and when i say love
and when i say here
and when i stay up   stray up esoteric and sad

sitting splintered
the pressure is now

lyric 3.9

so much descends on
something to insert
something splintered and swollen
and real

so much for metaphor
the sickly insert persona here

sucking on a ball point
discipline implicit in the scene
dreaming modes of dream
revolting and re-sending the
still fracture of insert trope

here
depend on it
descend on it

lyric 4

confident in you when you don't speak
or even breathe and even more confident that you
won't dream and a pristine death will court you
i can read you like a hymnal, your patented moans

you are pouring out into empty streets
into late night esoteric binges and regrets
into downpours, imaginary moors
hollow homes, damp pages
always somewhere   in order to bury something

waiting for you in the density of language
confident you won't show up
at least not wholly   you are spilling over anyone that will have you

confident and spent

lyric 4.1

this is tasteless   i'm stuck in bed
hypergravity
dispensable in pill form
      eyes rolled crossed or shut
shadowing tidal under the dark star's gaze
blinds drawn

a drone making eyes
at the covered window

spectacular dust patterns
webs draped on a bed
this is the truest movement
tasteless and dislinear

a drone raising an eyebrow
draping himself over the
lattice

sick

lyric 4.2

unfolding in
eternal parking lots

on the escalator ascending problematically toward the nuclear family
in countless malls you sprawl

the escalators trick you
because you let them

directionless and twitching   surrounded by fake foliage
lured by movement
escalating sentience

choking on "i do"
plunged out of a domestic drip

lyric 4.3

welcome to that moment when your
lexicon falters and your
delicate frame is filled with
one unspeakable question
that has to do with everything

in the silence of the sick
epiphanic stream
you begin to sublimate
you begin to forget
you begin the process
of becoming self-parental

anything tangential is swept
under the stars you begin to ignore

and you waste the remainder of your formative years writing sonnets

sonnet 1

      The static of a metered life in some
old verse or other is strangely recognized
by the twitching man in every chartered street:
the silent william who documents, sighs
and comes to see his life in breathless hymn
unmetered and deluded by any truth.
How sweet to trill the sickly song of youth.
How sick to see convention in a dream.
            Yet I am boundless when I feel the innocent
texts that touch and sin their way to sight.
I cannot be confined by what is spent
in endless nights by catatonic light.
And in london, william blake has wandered true
because a lonely ginsberg asked him to.

sonnet 1.01

perfectly alone and still is this son
syntactically estranged at evening's end
decorative, deranged, and just for once
he would like to believe in the text he sends
across the vitriolic sky through telephone
wires, and to another sickly son alone
he sighs, it is impossible to transmit
such displaced sentiment, and though
the world is a scripted mirror stage show
the sickly son remains too sure and split:
twinned on a ledge, under sheets, uninvolved
the words that fail to rise are bound to fall
     with language lost, the bedsit boys are ill
the two sad sons are sitting, musing still

section 2
semisorry

trapped in the pale subjunctive
—Catherine Hunter

semisorry

i'm semisorry for keeping you awake last night   i saw you twitch, heard you moan, felt your insane breath dance across my body

i'm semisorry for the last ditch lovers sucking face on the sidewalk like professional cynics

i'm semisorry for this silence that disperses itself between thoughts

i'm semisorry for discursive structures that i try to impose on our domestic landscape

i'm semisorry for sitcoms   i felt a laugh track thrumming underneath me as i reached for my pen

i'm semisorry for the pain i cause while sleeping through the most emotive sections of your speech

i'm semisorry for the ideology i am in and therefore out of touch

i'm semisorry for an era that defines itself with a past participle stroke of the pen

i'm semisorry for living when i'm not sure if i am

i'm semisorry always in relation to you with your ever-present ambience and your canonical resonance as "lover"

i'm semisorry for what is indeterminate and what will be

i'm semisorry for waking and waking again in a city that will never ask me a question

i'm semisorry for the dissatisfaction

i'm semisorry for anything and everything i can and will get my hands on i'm semisorry for what i need:

i need attention deficit narratives
and a sense of agency now

somewhat sick of the metonymy of naming
i'm much more interested in the possibilities that lie
i need to shame you
i need to participate
in the grandiose self-shunning

i need to vandalize the pastoral haunts
of some old hacking poets

and i'm somewhat sick
but i have infinite prescriptions
which can provide artificial
light

i am photosensitive

i need a sense of grounding
between the ellipsis and the ellipse
i need some kind of new eclipse ...

i'm semisorry for the distractions that are as disturbing as last night's
insomniac economy and the distractions that are not

and now
with the infinite noise
of montreal collapsing
into exaggerated storefronts

the entire metropolis folding itself
inward like an existential epiphany
revealed through a silent montage
in slow motion

and now in the reverse unpacking
of a multiple negation dream

i am truly semisorry

i am semisorry again for everything
i cannot explain, whimpering
"it is never completely my fault"
as i stand still, wavering and versing
in an emotive trance to the pedestrian shadows

and most of all, with the utmost partial sincerity
i'm semisorry for what follows

i'm semisorry so semisorry that i was such a fool

heliotrope

i will not present for you
an allusion filled
ode to determinism
with verbiage overflowing
like the vernal red river

this is the heliotrope i know
what you're thinking
elliptical
anti-flower
fluorescence
hurdling itself around
itself

and a difficult heliotrope like
attention deficit economies
yet pretty, dismissive missile

a heliotrope
and an anthropocentric twitch
language is a technology
discursive, abstract and
life weary

a historical tragedy
that plays on and on

the curious hybridity of the heliotrope
the genetic manipulation
trance inducing morphology

the trance of automatic writing
the fluid static blasphemous trance of action
inscriptions of immaculate density
that only wish to say
"i was here"

resonant electrical surge
and through words chronically electronic
what about the technologies of collective individuation?
should i write apocalyptic fear?
what a turbulent age
what an apparition
conjured up by our own senses
suicidal simulacra
dancing in pixels

heliocentric—
isotropic
the universe unfolding
from this notion
and so expanding
like bliss

a heliotrope is a plant with small fragrant purple flowers
[i just looked it up]

vocal texts thrum
in elliptical dreams
a heliotrope abstracting itself

lament

call us up
and have our heads lopped off
in a perverse synchronicity
against the backdrop
of a starry cosmogonic sky

in my own sick way
i admire you

i'm exactly like you
only i fear deeper
in a realm of meta-fear
i also fear god
only i fear that
he plays favourites and
i cannot negotiate this fear
and sadly
god does not exist
without you

and i won't fear someday
because i won't feel a thing

ode to my valium

incessantly doting on me
you are mildly encouraging
you ruin my posture
i'm generally indifferent to
you in me endlessly
leisure class drug
you are confused
and perhaps a little bitter
it's not what you are
it's what you signify:
there's no one home
the windows are coated
in a creamy beige pastel
a relationship weathers
everything is singular
sedated and fabulous
a medication in need
of medication

pharmacy

confessional phantom approaches the counter

      under pervasive fluorescence he asks for an extension

he shuffles in a consumer trance
    the patter of pills
the heat of everyone's eyes
    the self-loathing

the world is a decorative failure
    the urban clatter
the industry
    the fear of waking up

the dedication of every waking moment

    to the pursuit of sleep and sleeping pills

the urban pharmacies are open twenty-four hours
    the confessional phantom has a cabinet filled
with tireless dreams
    they cringe and twitch
as the days begin to long to end

he lives within spitting distance of his pharmacy

history

silent and salient cloak room mornings
     the snow lazily melting off our boots   the irrational violent
thrusts haunting our surroundings   the children breathe in the
air the breath of demons
     and the day is framed in the catatonic chatter of the cloak room
the sexual mythologies dispersing in whispers   the sickly order of
things   monstrous parkas sprawling on the floor

this is history

and a teacher waxes parasitic over an entire region
     schools stand erect, sighing like landmarks
and to the east, under an urban veil
     a poet sighs, transcendent and still

metaflow

let us flow then
you and me
problematically suburban
in an indecipherable urban scene

and the evening is revised across the sky
like modernist novocaine

we do live here

and it is nice
to feel up home
sometimes

let us wait
then me and you
we were never meant not to be in this world
with all of its sickly vegetation

with heliotropes
sprouting out of unconsciousness
and procreation presenting itself
as the ultimate practical joke

the two of us
under the shock treatment sky
we make poetry
and gurgle in bliss
unaesthetic
and hopelessly political
       hopelessly internal

remember the last time

remember the last time we freudian slipped together
and you wrote to me about negative space and the dimensional aspect
of the page?

remember the last time we didn't have to be together but we did?

remember
brutal remembrances—
childhood,
living,
etc?

remember the last time we vandalized
and walked across the history of the city
and tossed about ideas
with no regard for the ideas themselves?

slip

i test words
in your backlane
while your parents
sleep under the
insistent
lullaby of
a clicking
motion sensor

following the
accidental
mapping of oil
leaks i enter

trampling your
garden i

tripping on
parental shadows i

slipping in the i
the persona sighs

thinking about it:
drawn toward getting caught

throwing rocks
like insults
at your window

sprinting
against the
cultural
imperatives

i had the longest dream last night
you were there with the dark stars muttering my name like a curse

i was drowning in our failure for an infinite while
and i stitched a document of self-loathing i pricked myself awake

we whispered in sickening errors
[and we were half wrong]

across the comical fractured country i glimpsed
you glinting that suicide smile

that punctuation of yours trips me up
to the point where i'm no longer
in any syntax

who knows if the pills will ever work
or ever did work

my dream was domestic and funereal
you were there being you
inserting punctuation, sighing ...

perhaps you uttered my name like a insult
while my dream slept in

were you
trying to catch
me unconscious
with your doting needle?

you stitch us as artificial
losing the needle in me
or in my words

pacing between each breath
the places we lived are unravelling

my dreams are blistered
      my word

christened as a slip
with a right hook
hailed into performance
here i am failing falling
slipping between the seams
at recess time

not seeming quite like slip—
singular under the unseen stars
but you have always been plural
haven't you slip?

deep in the jargon of september i come to you
on the eve of employment
the wretched capital sun rises
a fine dust settles

and this is the only secret
i will let slip:

every year is formative

waxing deep on your suburban driveway
or deeper still in the language that
fails to conjure you up

i am developing in and out of slippage
the dreams sit sighing
the world sprawls out

i am developing bedsores
yet developing

we are who we are because
we can slip together
and write our way out
or stitch ourselves to home
and we recognize the
difference

we can lock ourselves in
somewhere
and be as discursive
as we want
be plural
and forget
to pack
our pills
develop
see what happens

i had to become an academic
[i don't like people, only words or dreams]

so dream you sickly academic
implode some codes or simply implode
because there are too many of you
asserting your worth
and slipping

poor slip
invoking dormant diction
claiming truth in fiction
dream or sedate yourself permanently

you might be missed
but only in theory

and if i don't seem sick enough
be patient
i am an abject dream
waiting to happen

my eyes roll with wonder
at the stillness

coerce me with a pact
dream me into mind slits
emote incisions

interpellate me

are you chronically displaced?
are your eyes stapled shut like mine?

you know this unkind binding
i know you know how it feels
to slip

vendor

shut your trap and let's go to the vendor
this evening is cursed with the myth of an ether%
dispensing electromagnetic truth, keeping things still
this river is fluxing hydroelectric static
you will never really know where you are

but winter can save you so
wrap yourself around this pause
this hail of breath,
the frigid billowing air
the frostbite on your lips
would you please shut up
and let me finish*

your life:
this sliver is only a temporary
fracture between your skin
and the ether you are in
this payroll is laced
this taste is spliced—
acrid, intangible
twinned on the tongue

i can't hear you and for this i thank you
this poetic movement is typically sad+
plural in the singular street underdressed
in this winter with this twelve pack and
a map that never works
don't say a word
write back

%   read 'anything that governs'
*   read 'implode'
+   read 'poetic'

unfinished poem#

\#   read 'cowardly act'

immaculate worming

immaculate worming through pedestrians

i hear the classists and casualists creaking in their spectacular coffins

consumers selecting this or that and i slide, melancholy and singular

from outside this customer ethic it is possible to establish alternate economies of dreaming

to transcend or whatever   a diversion slither through dirt

some nights the rain makes me social and i ascend to the street

to be trampled is an absolute joy

blooming

mosquitos are blooming in the thatch of thought
that spreads outward from the glimpse
and inward, unfurling in the parasitic mind
let's participate in the splicing of self
by placing products back on the shelf
or perhaps simply come in the moist spasm of weather

stealing moments in shopping carts
you and i and everything burrowed in our skin
we are trope stealing and dealing   feeling perfectly at home
home is where you are bitten, stung or named
ticks are slipping into something more
comfortable, readying themselves for an evening
of urban bliss

floral

where is that ink-stained floral print blouse
you borrowed from your mother's closet?

everyday you are losing your self in
synthetic fabric, in sleep
that just won't do

where are those sequined letters
i mistook for stars?

everyday, i am losing my self in
dark leisure on cheap parchment

mount royal cemetery—

reclined on children's gravestones
palimpsests
we squinted and inferred
margins, letters

you gave me names for trees and seeds and weeds and flowers
they all escape me now

except "black-eyed susan"

i gave you names for phobias, pharmaceuticals, theories
you claimed them as sublimated signs

reclined in a torrid ocean of neglected grass
and weeds calmed by a lack of fear

which seeds are these?

take this home and press it
stitch it into me

your eyes shut tight
still, off-white petals
impenetrable fabric
deflecting weather

that blouse—

if you find it
can i borrow it?

i know it won't fit

soundtracking

i'm calling you toward this door, this vial of pills and these utility bills
it's very nice inside today—
very little windchill, just frail breath, indiscrete and dis-settling

and in the hallowed home
i'm soundtracking
the story of missing you
with my muted voice

this door opens only for you [or anyone who can be read as "you"]

but
i'm never home
unless i'm freezing

however
i'm never home at all these days unless that glimpse takes me there

yet
it's very nice to feel at home wherever you are, rolling your eyes, slipping out of tune, dying in palliative bed under a minor chord sequence, thrift shopping for a shroud

if you come home soon, i can introduce you to your ghost— she has been stealing my clothes, performing our chores under a breathless dirge that i wrote while asleep

come home and
listen to what i fell into in your absence:

all that imaginary reverb and acid and your ghost still chimes in at times with trebled harmony like a window that captures the howl of wind and never opens
like a hinge that whines a pale whine

"it was lovely just waiting"

walking home from mile-end
around what we call a mountain
glancing at an illuminated hierarchy
projected on a building

the only problem with beauty is to gaze upon it
in an expansive waiting room or just waiting

montreal is looking lovely with its illuminated
commerce emblems frozen in the sky, immovable stars
sucking on the oxygen of the city

and we are breathing in halogen
and freon and shoe-gazing our way home
the ATMs are huddled together
like shivering street kids, fluorescent eyes

when i am asked
what it was like
to choke my way through
this vast, polite, sickly, amnesiac history
i will say "it was lovely just waiting"

freon

i want it cold
colder than that moment you said never

a city, a perverse lexicon and
a cheap, lit-up cross on the top of a hill

out of the freon ambience and onto an uneven street
standing still, hailing

the cab driver asks me if i got any "action"
montreal is full of action

every belligerent pedestrian
every low lit secret
whispers action

whisper appliance and then think about that word
whisper pedestrian

straining to whisper, pliant and so
listening, willing to form

i like to spend my time
where there is frigidity imposed

i want it

cold, narrow, claustrophobic street
just on the left   no action
thank you

whisper traction inside, the curtains asleep, freon at work
cold, dry air and a telephone

on an unsoft futon slipping into
pliancy

winter is listening

winter is listening to you unfold on the hardwood
winter is listening to my head hit the headboard

to my filtered whisper, to your unconscious moan, into to the hiss of muted traffic

you curl up like burnt paper and i stay closed off, bedridden, thinking in slow motion

across the barricaded expanse of the city, citizens trample thawing lawns, insects hum in subversive frequencies, the streets erode in a pathetic whine, and st. denis wakes up late and stretches out like an inpatient left out in the hallway

postscript

In a sense, *resume drowning* is a response to my first collection, *hover*. *hover* celebrated the narcotic possibilities of poetry. Through rhetorical and poetic devices, I attempted to achieve an exuberance of verse. In this book I am engaging in performative melancholy and working in the tradition of the lyric. As opposed to hovering, I am drowning; and at times I need to take a quick break from drowning—I resurface, edit and muse, and then resume drowning. Throughout these poems I am engaging intertextually with Emily Dickinson, bp Nichol, Adrienne Rich, Steven Patrick Morrissey, Catherine Hunter, Mary di Michele, Stevie Smith, Sylvia Plath and of course Sappho. The true inspiration for this collection is the poem "Not Waving but Drowning" by Stevie Smith.

I desire texts that are confessional, emotive, playful. When my poems seem to delve into the most abject melancholy, they are also at their most hyperbolic. These poems celebrate the lyric and if they are successful, they apply theory to the lyric as well. Many of these poems are informed by the notion of place: Transcona, Winnipeg and Montreal inhabit these poems as I have inhabited these places and consider all three of them home.

I wish to thank my family, rob mclennan, Joe Blades, Rob Budde, Catherine Hunter, Clive Holden, Geoff Lansdell, Sarah Steinberg, Kate Hall, Leigh Scharnik, Chris Charney, Chandra Mayor, Mary di Michele, Chrystal Staver, Manon Christina Palassio, Terry Watts, and my partner, Tara Flanagan.

A Selection of Our Titles

A Fredericton Alphabet (John Leroux) photos, architecture	1-896647-77-4	14.95
Avoidance Tactics (Sky Gilbert) drama	1-896647-50-2	15.88
Bathory (Moynan King) drama	1-896647-36-7	14.95
Break the Silence (Denise DeMoura) poetry	1-896647-87-1	13.95
Combustible Light (Matt Santateresa) poetry	0-921411-97-9	12.95
Crossroads Cant (Mary Elizabeth Grace, Mark Seabrook, Shafiq, Ann Shin. Joe Blades, editor) poetry	0-921411-48-0	13.95
Cuerpo amado/Beloved Body (Nela Rio; Hugh Hazelton, translator) poetry	1-896647-81-2	15.88
Dark Seasons (Georg Trakl; Robin Skelton, trans.) poetry	0-921411-22-7	10.95
Day of the Dog-tooth Violets (Christina Kilbourne) novel	1-896647-44-8	17.76
for a cappuccino on Bloor (kath macLean) poetry	0-921411-74-X	13.95
Great Lakes logia (Joe Blades, ed.) art & writing anthology	1-896647-70-7	16.82
Heaven of Small Moments (Allan Cooper) poetry	0-921411-79-0	12.95
Herbarium of Souls (Vladimir Tasic) short fiction	0-921411-72-3	14.95
I Hope It Don't Rain Tonight (Phillip Igloliorti) poetry	0-921411-57-X	11.95
Jive Talk: George Fetherling in Interviews and Documents (George Fetherling; editor Joe Blades)	1-896647-54-5	13.95
Manitoba highway map (rob mclennan) poetry	0-921411-89-8	13.95
Notes on drowning (rob mclennan) poetry	0-921411-75-8	13.95
Paper Hotel (rob mclennan) poetry	1-55391-004-4	17.95
Peppermint Night (Vanna Tessier) poetry	1-896647-83-9	13.95
Railway Station (karl wendt) poetry	0-921411-82-0	11.95
Reader Be Thou Also Ready (Robert James) novel	1-896647-26-X	18.69
resume drowning (Jon Paul Fiorentino) poetry	1-896647-94-4	15.95
Rum River (Raymond Fraser) fiction	0-921411-61-8	16.95
Shadowy Technicians: New Ottawa Poets (ed. rob mclennan) poetry	0-921411-71-5	16.95
Singapore (John Palmer) drama	1-896647-85-5	15.88
Song of the Vulgar Starling (Eric Miller) poetry	0-921411-93-6	14.95
Speaking Through Jagged Rock (Connie Fife) poetry	0-921411-99-5	12.95
Starting from Promise (Lorne Dufour) poetry	1-896647-52-9	13.95
Tales for an Urban Sky (Alice Major) poetry	1-896647-11-1	13.95
The Longest Winter (Julie Doiron, Ian Roy) photos, fiction	0-921411-95-2	18.69
These Are My Elders (Chad Norman; Heather Spears, ill.)	1-896647-74-X	13.95
The Sweet Smell of Mother's Milk-Wet Bodice (Uma Parameswaran) fiction	1-896647-72-3	13.95
This Day Full of Promise: Poems Selected and New (Michael Dennis, rob mclennan (editor) poetry	1-896647-48-0	15.88
Túnel de proa verde/Tunnel of the Green Prow (Nela Rio; Hugh Hazelton, translator) poetry	0-921411-80-4	13.95
What Was Always Hers (Uma Parameswaran) fiction	1-896647-12-X	17.95

www.brokenjaw.com hosts our current catalogue, submissions guidelines, manuscript award competitions, booktrade sales representation and fulfilment information. Directly from us, all individual orders must be prepaid. All Canadian orders must add 7% GST/HST (Canada Customs and Revenue Agency Number: 12489 7943 RT0001). Broken Jaw Press eBooks (in PDF format) of selected titles are available at http://www.PublishingOnline.com.

BROKEN JAW PRESS, Box 596 Stn A, Fredericton NB E3B 5A6, Canada